KW-757-788

EVANGELICALS AND THE OXFORD MOVEMENT

Rev. John Carrick, MA
Minister of Cheltenham Evangelical Free Church

EVANGELICAL PRESS OF WALES
on behalf of
THE EVANGELICAL LIBRARY, LONDON

© John Carrick, 1984
First published 1984
ISBN 1 85049 000 7

All rights reserved. No part of this publication may be reproduced, stored in a retrieval system, or transmitted, in any form or by any means, electronic, mechanical, photo-copying, recording or otherwise, without the prior permission of the Evangelical Press of Wales.

Cover illustration: Martyrs' Memorial, Oxford
(from J. C. Ryle's *Light from Old Times*)

This lecture, the Annual Lecture of the Evangelical Library for 1983, was originally delivered on Monday, 4 July 1983, at Westminster Chapel, London.

Published by the Evangelical Press of Wales, Bryntirion, Bridgend
Mid Glamorgan CF31 4DX on behalf of the
Evangelical Library, 78a Chiltern St., London W1M 2HB.
Printed by the Bridgend Printing Co. Ltd., Bridgend, Mid Glam.

Preface

The Evangelical Library owes its existence to the vision of the late Geoffrey Williams, who in the period between the two world wars built up (and so saved from neglect and destruction) a remarkable collection of Protestant and Puritan literature. First housed at Beddington, Surrey, in 1943, with the active encouragement of the late Dr Martyn Lloyd-Jones, it was moved to Central London, and the Library in its present form was born.

Much extended, and ever growing, the collection is now housed at 78a Chiltern Street, London W1M 2HB, where its resources and borrowing facilities are available to all its members. There are also numerous branches, both in the United Kingdom and overseas.

The Evangelical Library Lecture, on a subject of interest to Protestants, is delivered annually. Full liberty in expressing his opinions is extended to the speaker invited to give it.

THE EVANGELICAL LIBRARY LECTURES

1952*	E. F. Kevan	The Puritan doctrine of conversion
1953*	John Murray	Reformation principles
1954*	F. F. Bruce	The sure mercies of David
1955*	Edwin Lewis	The Puritans and the Seventh of Romans
1956*	Iain Murray	The faith of the English Reformers
1957*	Ralph E. Ford	The lesser-known works of John Bunyan
1958	Edward J. Young	Jesus Christ the Servant of the Lord
1959*	James Cossar	Contending for the faith
1960*	Eifion Evans	Revivals: their rise progress and achievements
1961*	G. N. M. Collins	Samuel Rutherford
1962*	D. M. Lloyd-Jones	1662-1962: From Puritanism to Non-conformity
1963	A. Skevington Wood	William Grimshaw of Haworth
1964*	John Murray	Calvin as theologian and expositor
1965	W. J. Grier	Hus and Farel
1966	Wilbur M. Smith	The endless stream of books
1967*	R. J. Graham	Martin Luther and his relevance for today
1968*	D. B. Knox	The Lord's Supper in early English reformed writings
1969	D. P. Kingdon	Training for the ministry
1970	Hywel R. Jones	Thomas Cartwright, 1535-1603
1971	Graham Harrison	Dr John Gill and his teaching
1972	Iain Murray	John Knox
1973	NO LECTURE	
1974	S. M. Houghton	Isaac Watts
1975*	Hywel R. Jones	Samuel Tregelles, 1813-1875
1976*	R. T. Kendall	The influence of Calvin and Calvinism upon the American heritage
1977	Andrew A. Davies	The Moravian revival of 1727 and some of its consequences
1978	Paul E. G. Cook	Augustus Toplady the saintly sinner
1979	John E. Marshall	Thomas Scott and 'The force of truth'
1980	A. Sinclair Horne	Richard Cameron: martyr, revolutionary and preacher, 1648-1680
1981	Peter Lewis	Philip Henry, 1631-1696: from palace to pulpit
1982	Frederick and Elizabeth Catherwood	Martyn Lloyd-Jones: the man and his books
1983	John Carrick	Evangelicals and the Oxford Movement

* = out of print

Evangelicals and the Oxford Movement

'FROM beginnings so small, from elements of thought so fortuitous, with prospects so unpromising, the Anglo-Catholic party suddenly became a power in the National Church, and an object of alarm to her rulers and friends . . . . In a very few years a school of opinion was formed, fixed in its principles, indefinite and progressive in their range; and it extended itself into every part of the country.' It was thus that the presiding genius of the Oxford Movement, John Henry Newman, described in later years the drama that had convulsed the religious world over a period of some twelve years, from 1833 to 1845. Variously known as Tractarianism or Puseyism, the drama of the Oxford Movement involved a remarkable rise in the fortunes and influence of the Anglo-Catholic party within our shores and beyond, the repercussions and reverberations of which are still with us today, 150 years later. [1]

The Political Climate

What, then, were the circumstances under which the Oxford Movement arose? Well, it was in fact a political impetus, even a political crisis—'a revolution in the relations between Church and State'—which gave opportunity to the rise of the Oxford Movement and which provided its occasion. The era was one of reform, and the times were those of agitation and change. The Catholic Emancipation of 1829, for instance, now allowed Roman Catholics to sit in the Parliament at Westminster. Again, in the following year,

1830, the Liberal-Whigs came to power after a long period of Tory ascendancy, whilst two years later, in 1832, the triumph of the Reform Bill further weakened the Tory traditions upon which, in the minds of High Churchmen, the authority of the Church seemed to rest politically. Furthermore, the Irish Church of 1833, with its suppression of ten out of twenty-two Irish Bishoprics—and that in defiance of the opinion of the Established Church—was the final confirmation in the minds of certain High Churchmen that this was the hour of peril for the English Church. Thus when on Sunday, 14 July 1833, John Keble, Professor of Poetry at the University of Oxford, preached the Assize Sermon in the University Pulpit, he took as his theme the alarmist one of 'National Apostasy'. 'If it be true anywhere', said Keble, 'that such enactments are forced on the Legislature by public opinion, is APOSTASY too hard a word to describe the temper of that nation?' To Keble and other High Churchmen it was 'the grossest Erastianism', it was 'Erastian sacrilege', that a civil government—and a Whig government at that!—should seek to lay hands on the Established Church. Moreover, this sacrilegious invasion of the rights of the Church aroused the fears of Tory High Churchmen that the new Liberal-Whig Government might engage in further intrusion and further high-handed changes with regard to the Established Church. Thus Keble and his friends felt that it was now time to assert that even if the Church were disestablished, even if there were a complete separation between Church and State, and even if the State followed the example of the United States of America and became outwardly and constitutionally indifferent to religion, the Church of England still retains a claim upon the allegiance of Englishmen precisely because this Church teaches Catholic truth, and as such manifests itself to be the authorized and commissioned agent of Christ and his apostles to the people of this country. Thus John Keble, in his sermon of 14 July 1833, issued a call for devotion to 'the cause of the Apostolical Church in these realms'. For Keble and his fellow High Churchmen, the authority of the Church did not rest upon the authority of the State; the Church possessed a divine authority whatever the State may do, and that divine authority lay for them in the doctrine of the apostolic succession. [2]

John Keble's Assize Sermon of 14 July 1833 marks, then, the commencement of the Oxford Movement. John Henry Newman, for his part, informs us in his *Apologia* that he 'ever considered and kept the day, as the start of the religious movement of 1833'. In the course of the next eight years some 90 'Tracts' were published, issuing in the main from the pens of John Henry Newman, Edward Bouverie Pusey, John Keble, Richard Hurrell Froude, Charles Marriott and Isaac Williams, all of whom, significantly, (with the one exception of Isaac Williams) were fellows of Oriel College, Oxford. The first of these Tracts was published by Newman on 9 September 1833, and in this Tract Newman reiterated Keble's emphasis upon the apostolic succession. 'I fear we have neglected', he wrote, 'the real ground on which our authority is built—OUR APOSTOLICAL DESCENT.' Bishops, he asserted, were the 'SUCCESSORS OF THE APOSTLES', and ministers of the Church of England were appointed the 'assistants, and in some sense representatives' of the bishops by the laying on of hands. There was, Newman contended, this unbroken historic succession, this lineal descent from the apostles themselves which gave authentic standing to the Church of England within Christendom. [3]

This, then, was the Tractarians' initial counterblast against what they perceived to be Liberal aggression and the scourge of Erastianism—a scourge which Newman described as 'that *double usurpation*, the interference of the Church in temporals, of the State in spirituals'. Moreover, the Tractarian mind tended to perceive a connection between Erastianism and Liberalism. 'With Froude,' wrote Newman, 'Erastianism,—that is the union of Church and State,—was the parent, or if not the parent, the serviceable and sufficient tool, of liberalism. Till that union was snapped, Christian doctrine never could be safe.' [4]

The Tractarian mind of 1833 was, then, strongly anti-Erastian. Indeed, Newman himself asserted some thirty years later that 'those anti-Erastian views of Church polity . . . were one of the most prominent features of the Tractarian movement'. However, there were other factors involved besides the political situation in England. July 1830, for instance, had witnessed the downfall of the Restoration monarchy in France—a new revolution, this, which appeared to be directed against the Church as well as against the Throne, and which sent a shudder of alarm through conservative circles everywhere. 'The French', wrote Newman to Hurrell Froude, 'are an awful people . . . . This revolution seems to me the triumph of irreligion . . . . The effect of this miserable French affair will be great in England.' Its effect on Newman himself was certainly considerable, for he himself tells us that when in Algiers during his Mediterranean journey of 1832-3, he could not bring himself to look at the tricolour on a French vessel there, and that when he was passing through Paris, he kept indoors for the whole period of 24 hours, such was his evident sensitivity to the pollution of Liberalism.[5]

Liberalism

However, it was not merely the politics of France which concerned the Tractarians; it was also the theology of Germany. For if the age was one of political reform and revolution in England and France, then it was equally one of theological innovation and reconstruction in Germany. Friedrich Schleiermacher, the man widely regarded as 'the father of modern theology', had founded a whole new era in theology. It was an era of theological reinterpretation and reconstruction; the era of liberal theology had already begun, and Schleiermacher himself was now at his life's end.

Thus, as conservatives both in their politics and in their theology, the Tractarians were opposed to Liberalism in all its forms. As conservatives they feared the undermining of authority and tradition, they feared the destruction of consensus. New ideas were being propagated and filled the air; there was this 'licence of opinion' abroad, this 'false liberty of thought'; there was this 'free market in opinions'.

Political Liberalism and religious Liberalism were thus identified in their minds, even confused, and were regarded as utterly anti-Christian. 'The more serious thinkers among us', wrote Newman, 'are used . . . to regard the spirit of Liberalism as the characteristic of the destined Antichrist.' Newman's battle, then, was with Liberalism; he felt that a stand had to be made against the liberal menace; and the essence of that menace lay in the 'anti-dogmatic principle'. 'The vital question was', wrote Newman, 'how were we to keep the Church from being liberalized?' A counter-movement was clearly needed, he felt, and the fundamental principle of that counter-movement would be 'the principle of dogma'. The Tractarians would take refuge in the dogmas of the ancient and undivided Church.[6]

Why was it, however, that the leaders of the Oxford Movement did not take refuge in the Evangelical principle of 'Scripture alone'? Why did they not, as a counterblast to theological Liberalism, reassert the divine authority of the Holy Scriptures alone, the great *sola scriptura* principle of the Reformation? For Newman the answer to this question lay in the connection which he perceived between the Reformation and Liberalism itself. 'The spirit of lawlessness', he wrote, 'came in with the Reformation, and Liberalism is its offspring.' 'Rationalism', asserted Newman, 'is the great evil of the day . . . . I am more certain that the Protestant [spirit], which I oppose, leads to infidelity, than that which I recommend, leads to Rome.' Newman was in fact tragically wrong on both scores here. On the one hand he overstates his case considerably when he asserts that the Protestant spirit leads to infidelity and that Liberalism is the offspring of the Reformation. For whilst Evangelicals are prepared to concede that both political and theological Liberalism were ultimate by-products of the liberating spirit of the Reformation, they emphasize that theological Liberalism or Rationalism, for its part, was a corruption, and not a legitimate development, of the principles of the Reformation; they are under no obligation historically to posit anything more than this indirect connection between them. On the other hand,

Newman's own secession to Rome in 1845 proves that the pathway of Catholic dogma does lead irresistibly in the direction of Rome.[7]

In Newman's mind there was, however, this strange identification between the spirit of Evangelicalism and the spirit of Liberalism. 'I thought little of the Evangelicals as a class', Newman wrote. 'I thought they played into the hands of the Liberals.' The connecting link in his mind was the principle or right of private judgement—a principle or right claimed both by Evangelicals and Liberals. Here again, however, Newman is guilty of failing to distinguish between things that differ; for the principle of private judgement as exercised by the Bereans, who 'searched the scriptures daily, whether those things were so', is quite different from the principle of private judgement as exercised by Friedrich Schleiermacher, who searched the Scriptures regularly and sifted out those things that offended. In the former case the right of private judgement was exercised by men under authority; in the latter case it was exercised by a man who had cut loose from external authority. Newman, however, failed to make this vital distinction, and as a result he tended to speak of Evangelicals and Evangelicalism in a very dismissive way, as if Evangelicalism were directly responsible for Liberalism! Thus it was not a return to Evangelical doctrine which Newman and his fellow Tractarians urged; it was a return to the dogmas of the early centuries, the dogmas of the 'Church Catholic and Apostolic'.[8]

The Romantic Spirit

There was, however, one further crucial factor in the rise of the Oxford Movement, and that was the spirit of the age. Newman himself concedes this when in his *Apologia*, he speaks of 'a spirit afloat'. 'It was not so much a movement', he contended, 'as a spirit afloat; it was within us, rising up in hearts where it was least expected.' There was a particular climate, a particular atmosphere that prevailed—it was the Romantic environment of the day. Indeed, in his *Apologia*, Newman specifically mentions four of the great literary figures of the time—Sir Walter Scott, Robert Southey, William Wordsworth and Samuel Taylor Coleridge. It was these men, Newman asserted, who prepared the imagination of the nation for the reception of Catholic truth. 'Walter Scott', he wrote, 'turned men's minds in the direction of the middle ages.' Scott stimulated an interest in the medieval and the Gothic, an interest in antiquarianism. The Romantic mind, living in the Railway Age, the age of the Industrial Revolution, felt at odds with the present, and felt this nostalgia for the past, the remote, and was greatly attracted by Scott's enchantment with the Middle Ages. The longing for 'a deeper philosophy', 'a higher philosophy', was part of the spirit of the age, so that the spirit of Tractarianism was, in Newman's words, 'an adversary in the air, . . . unapproachable and incapable of being grasped, as being the result of causes far deeper than political or other visible agencies, the spiritual awakening of spiritual wants'. [9]

What, then, was the essence of the Romantic spirit? Feeling, emotion, the cult of sensibility, sincerity, intensity, freedom, spontaneity, self-expression, instinct, impulse, intuition, mystery, depth, imagination, fantasy, vision, wonder, reverence and awe—these are the notes which are of the essence of Romanticism. A dramatic reaction against the Enlightenment of the eighteenth century had set in, and the Romantic Movement was a vital part of that great swing of opinion against Reason—the cold and barren concept of Reason as taught by John Locke and accepted by the Age of the Enlightenment. Throughout Europe there had been this great revolt against reason, logic, philosophy and the empiricism of science. It was a 'flight from Reason', a protest against rationalism in both art and life, an 'almost universal turning from the head towards the heart'. Listen, for instance, to these lines from Wordsworth's poem 'The Tables Turned':

> One impulse from a vernal wood
> May teach you more of man,
> Of moral evil and of good,
> Than all the sages can.

Wordsworth is critical of 'our meddling intellect', he is critical of 'books', and instead he idealizes 'spontaneous wisdom', and Nature as our teacher. The influence of Wordsworth upon the spirit of the age during the first three decades of the nineteenth century had been considerable, and by the 1830s the stars of both Wordsworth and Coleridge in Cambridge were in the ascendant. The 1830s were 'the Romantic decade par excellence'.[10]

Now, it is most significant that the leading Tractarians were in fact poets. John Keble was of course Professor of Poetry at Oxford from 1831 to 1841. Isaac Williams would almost certainly have been Keble's successor as Professor of Poetry in 1841 but for the controversy created by his Tracts on 'Reserve'. Edward Pusey was regarded as the *doctor mysticus* of the Movement, whilst John Henry Newman's remarkable gift for writing haunting poetic prose was that of a genius. Listen to Newman's views on poetry: 'Poetry', he writes,

> does not address the reason, but the imagination and affections; it leads to admiration, enthusiasm, devotion, love. The vague, the uncertain, the irregular, the sudden, are among its attributes and sources. Hence it is that a child's mind is so full of poetry because he knows so little; and an old man of the world so devoid of poetry, because his experience of facts is so wide.

There is this typically Romantic trait—the idealization of a childlike or primitive view of the world—a view which is essentially poetic. 'Alas!' wrote Newman on another occasion, 'what are we doing all through life . . . but unlearning the world's poetry, and attaining to its prose!' It is this wistful idealization of poetry and of the poetical that is so striking and so significant here on Newman's part, for it is the wistful idealization of an essentially Romantic mind.[11]

Furthermore, the Romantic mind felt that the poet enjoyed a peculiar insight into reality, an intuitive perception of truth, even powers of divination. It was the imagination of the poet that enabled him to lift the veil upon reality. Listen for instance to William Blake:

> *One Power alone makes a Poet:*
> *Imagination, The Divine Vision.*[12]

The Romantic poet thus saw himself as a visionary—a visionary who, in his yearning for the infinite, was able by force of imagination to penetrate the veiled mysteries of the universe. All things, Coleridge once wrote, 'counterfeit infinity', and if all things 'counterfeit infinity', then everything can be taken as symbolical, as a type or a shadow of another world. Listen again to Coleridge:

> *For all that meets the bodily sense I deem*
> *Symbolical, one mighty alphabet*
> *For infant minds: and we in this low world*
> *Placed with our back to bright Reality,*
> *That we may learn with young unwounded ken*
> *The substance from its shadow.*

Now there can be no doubt but that Coleridge's influence upon Newman was considerable, despite their differences. Newman himself wrote on one occasion: 'Material phenomena are both the types and the instruments of real things unseen.' The natural world is regarded as an emblem of the unseen, spiritual world. David Newsome is thus quite correct when he writes that 'Newman's fellow-Romantics . . . saw in the finite world glimpses of infinity, through their power to read the symbolism or to exercise the poetic imagination.' It was this 'sacramentalism of nature and the world' which the Tractarians imbibed from the Romantics, and which explains to a very significant degree the deepening theological sacramentalism of the Oxford Movement. It was thus, wrote Newman, that Coleridge 'made trial of his age, . . . and succeeded in interesting its genius in the cause of Catholic truth.'[13]

There is, then, a natural coalescing between the spirit and ethos of Romanticism and the spirit and ethos of Catholicism. John Henry Newman himself virtually concedes this when he writes: 'The Church of Rome . . . alone, amid all the errors and evils of her practical system, has given free scope to the feelings of awe, mystery, tenderness, reverence, devotedness,

13

and other feelings which may be especially called Catholic.'
And a crucial part of this natural coalescing between the
Romantic spirit and the Catholic spirit is the symbolic and
sacramental world-view which unites them both. 'This
poetic strand', writes Professor Owen Chadwick, 'was part of
that symbolic and sacramental consciousness which formed
the deepest link . . . between Romanticism and Catholicism.'
John Henry Newman, despite his Evangelical background,
became a Catholic, and ultimately a Roman Catholic,
because he was by nature and by temperament a Romantic. [14]

The Tractarian Rule of Faith

We turn now, then, to the vital issue of the Tractarians'
Rule of Faith. Their appeal was not exclusively to the
Scriptures; it was also to 'Antiquity'. Their great emphasis
was avowedly and unashamedly upon Antiquity, Ancient
Religion, the Fathers, the Creeds, Apostolic Tradition, the
witness of the Primitive Church. It was here that authority lay
for the Tractarian mind. There was in the Tractarians this
distinct veneration and idealization of the past which
harmonized well with the backward glance of the Romantics.
Did not Newman himself, when describing the spirit of the
age, speak of 'the general need of something deeper and more
attractive, than what had offered itself elsewhere'? This, the
Tractarians felt, was to be found in the Catholic heritage of
the Fathers, and it is interesting and of significance to note
that the deep Platonism of the Fathers harmonized well with
the Neoplatonism of the Romantic mind. Thus whilst it is true
to say that the threat of Liberalism drove the Tractarians
back to the past by way of reaction, it is also true to say that
the charm of Romanticism lured them back to the past by way
of attraction. They took refuge in the teaching of the Fathers,
and clearly felt that they had now found a principle of
authority to which they could appeal. [15]

The influence of Dr Hawkins in this respect was
considerable. Newman's predecessor in the pulpit of St
Mary's, Dr Hawkins was later to become the Provost of Oriel
College, and it was from Dr Hawkins that Newman gained his

doctrine of Tradition. As an undergraduate Newman heard Dr Hawkins preach his famous sermon on the subject of Tradition, and it was a sermon which subsequently was to make a most serious impression upon him. 'Dr. Hawkins', wrote Newman,

> lays down a proposition, self-evident as soon as stated, to those who have at all examined the structure of Scripture, viz. that the sacred text was never intended to teach doctrine, but only to prove it, and that, if we would learn doctrine, we must have recourse to the formularies of the Church; for instance to the Catechism, and to the Creeds. He considers, that, after learning from them the doctrines of Christianity the inquirer must verify them by Scripture.

Thus Newman adopted, unquestioningly it seems, this idea from Dr Hawkins that it is the Church that teaches doctrine, whilst the Scriptures simply prove and verify the doctrine thus taught. We have here from the leader of the Oxford Movement a prime example of what William Cunningham described as 'that depreciation of the Scriptures, that denial of their fitness, because of their obscurity and alleged imperfection, to be a sufficient rule or standard of faith, which stamp so peculiar a guilt and infamy upon . . . Tractarianism'. The Scriptures are subordinated by the Tractarians into a position which is merely secondary, whilst the Creeds are elevated into a position which is primary. 'Whatever doctrine the primitive ages unanimously attest,' wrote Newman, 'whether by consent of the Fathers, or by Councils, or by the events of history, or by controversies . . . is to be received as coming from the Apostles.' 'The fundamental or essential doctrines are those which are contained in the Creed', he asserted. Thus Newman and the other Tractarians emphasized what they regarded as 'the original deposit' of Christian truth—a deposit which was to be found in the so-called 'orthodox consensus' and in which, they contended, all branches of the Church agreed.[16]

Clearly, then, the Tractarian Rule of Faith involved an open denial of the great *sola scriptura* principle of the

15

Protestant Reformation. Tradition was elevated by the Tractarians into a joint rule of faith. 'God's unwritten Word', 'the primitive, unwritten system', demanded for them the same reverence as His written Word. There was for them this double rule of faith—the Bible *and* Tradition. John Keble, for his part, clothed this idea in his own poetic language: 'Tradition and Scripture were at first two streams flowing down from the mountain of God, but their waters presently became blended, and it were but a vain and unpractical inquiry, to call upon every one who drinks of them to say, how much of the healing draught came from one source, and how much from the other'—an example, this, of a poetic and unscriptural analogy, dangerous at once for its poetry and its analogical reasoning. [17]

But how did the Tractarians endeavour to define 'Tradition' itself? Well, at this point they had recourse to the Rule of Vincentius of Lérins, formulated in AD 434—*'Quod semper, quod ubique, quod ab omnibus'* ('That which has *always* been believed, that which has been believed *everywhere*, and that which has been believed *by all men*'). John Keble was expressing the same idea when he spoke of 'Antiquity, Universality, Catholicity'. It was the idea of a universal consensus on dogma, the idea of 'catholic consent'; it was the old idea, familiar in the early centuries, of an 'orthodox consensus' which was regarded as normative; and it was via this consensus that the Tractarians felt they would recover for the Church the Catholic heritage which it had lost. [18]

The vital question, however, remains, and it is this: how valid and how practicable was this appeal to the orthodox consensus of the Fathers? William Goode, the most able and incisive Anglican assailant of Tractarian doctrine, pointed out that whilst the *theory* of the Tractarians was that 'catholic consent' only can be relied upon, that which they '*practically* rely upon to prove this consent is often the dictum of half a dozen Fathers'. In other words, there was this strong selective, indeed arbitrary, element in the Tractarian approach to the Fathers. Newman himself, during his years of personal crisis after 1841, came to acknowledge that 'after all we must

16

use private judgment upon Antiquity'. Moreover, William Goode pointed out quite correctly that 'the witness of Patristical Tradition . . . is of a discordant kind, and that even in fundamental points'. There are these mutual contradictions amongst the Fathers in that one Father destroys what another seeks to establish. Goode therefore contended, rightly, that the whole notion of a consentient testimony was 'a mere dream of the imagination'.[19]

What becomes, then, of the Rule of Vincentius which is so fundamental to the 'orthodox consensus' and the concept of 'catholic consent'? Well, at this point the Achilles' heel of this particular rule lies upon its very surface. It is a rule which appears to be completely oblivious to the power and tenacity of heresy. Jaroslav Pelikan, in *The Emergence of the Catholic Tradition*, writes that 'it was inconceivable to the exponents of the orthodox consensus that there could be any contradiction between Scripture properly interpreted and the tradition of the ancient fathers'. The mere possibility that heresy might be found lurking within the 'orthodox consensus' is dismissed *a priori* as being inconceivable. Such a position betokens both a naive underestimation of the depravity of man's heart and mind, and a naive overestimation of the providential preservation of pure doctrine. The result is that this Rule of Vincentius actually *fossilizes* any heresy that is widely accepted as truth. It is a rule which not only includes light and excludes darkness, it also includes darkness and excludes light. It sanctions, perpetuates and fossilizes ancient heresy as well as ancient orthodoxy. The ultimate effect of this rule, so fundamental to the concept of Tradition, is to *inject* the word of man into the Word of God and thus, like the traditions of Pharisaism, to make the Word of God of none effect. It is for this reason that Dr Merle d'Aubigné, in the course of a lecture given in 1842 entitled 'Geneva and Oxford', spoke of this whole concept of Tradition as being 'a species of rationalism'. It is one of the tragic ironies of the rise of the Oxford Movement that in fleeing from the rationalism of Germany, the Tractarians did but flee into the arms of a different rationalism—a

17

rationalism 'which introduces into Christian doctrine, as a rule, not the human reason of the present time, but the human reason of times past'.[20]

When we turn to the Creeds, however, it is a more subtle deficiency that we observe, namely the relative silence of the Creeds on certain vital doctrines. For whilst the Creeds are generally excellent as a summary of scriptural doctrine on the subjects of the Trinity and the Person of Christ, there is in them a comparative neglect with regard to the doctrines of anthropology and soteriology. The doctrines of grace are thrown into the background, and there is this great inadequacy and insufficiency with regard to the divine method of the justification of the sinner. As Dr W. G. T. Shedd emphasizes, the Creeds are 'inferior as to comprehensiveness'. There are these ancient omissions, these ancient deficiencies about them which render any return to the 'Ancient Religion' of the early centuries potentially dangerous since, as Dr Shedd rightly contends, 'there was no barrier, of a *theoretical* kind, to the entrance of . . . the legalistic theory of justification'. Evangelical Protestants, therefore, are quite entitled to point out that the very rise of the Oxford Movement within the bosom of the Church of England was in no small measure due to the defectiveness, inadequacy and insufficiency of the very Creeds to which the Tractarians so gladly appealed.[21]

The Doctrine of Justification

We turn now, then, to the subject of the divine method of the justification of the sinner—a subject of such vital importance that the Apostle Paul, in his epistle to the Galatians, pronounces the double anathema of God upon those who would fain pervert the doctrine of justification by faith alone in Christ. This was the doctrine which Martin Luther described as 'the article of the standing or the falling of the Church'; and yet it is also a doctrine upon which the Creeds of the early centuries are silent. Now it was to this biblical doctrine of justification by faith alone in the merits and the work of Jesus Christ that the Tractarians showed

18

considerable opposition. In 1843 a writer in the *British Critic* wrote of 'the soul-destroying heresy of Luther on the subject of Justification', whilst Newman, for his part, had come to reject the doctrine of imputed righteousness which, from his Evangelical days, he appears to have held from 1816 until 1826. He, like other Tractarians, felt that Evangelicalism bred mere antinomianism, and that the doctrine of justification by faith alone was therefore immoral because of this alleged result. Clearly Newman felt disillusioned by the low level of personal sanctification amongst Evangelicals. His great admiration for the Evangelical Thomas Scott was based upon the latter's 'bold unworldliness' and upon 'his resolute opposition to Antinomianism'. However, as far as Newman was concerned, Evangelicalism had lost the spirit of Thomas Scott and had succumbed both to worldliness and antinomianism. 'The Evangelical party itself', wrote Newman, 'seemed to have lost that simplicity and unworldliness which I admired so much in . . . Scott'. It was Newman's perception of defects amongst Evangelicals in this respect that constitutes one of the factors which drove him increasingly away from Evangelicalism and in the direction of Catholicism. [22]

However, if Newman regarded the Evangelical doctrine of justification as unsound and erroneous, it is also true to say that in the earlier years of the Oxford Movement he regarded the Roman Catholic doctrine of justification as defective. Thus in his *Lectures on Justification*, published in 1838, Newman sought to steer a middle course between the Protestant and Roman Catholic doctrines of justification. He sought to establish a *via media* doctrine of justification, an intermediate doctrine, a new synthesis which would, he felt, fuse into one new doctrine the primary aspects of both Protestantism and Roman Catholicism. These *Lectures* he therefore regarded as 'an Irenicon'; they had an irenic, even ecumenical, aim and purpose. 'Their drift', he wrote, 'is to show that there is little difference but what is verbal in the various views on justification whether found among Catholic or Protestant divines.' 'I wished to fill up a ditch, the work of man.' [23]

19

Newman contended, therefore, in his *Lectures* that 'Justification by faith' and 'Justification by obedience' are not 'opposite doctrines', but 'separate' and 'not at all inconsistent with each other'. He urged, indeed, that they are 'so compatible in themselves, that they may be held both at once, or indifferently, either the one or the other', as being 'but two modes of stating the same truth'. Again, he asserted that 'Justification by faith' and 'Justification by baptism' need not be opposed to one another, for 'baptism may be considered the instrument on God's part, faith on ours'. 'Baptism', he wrote, 'makes faith justifying.' Thus, whereas the method of the Scriptures on this vital doctrine is that of antithesis or contrast, Newman's method is that of synthesis. 'Justification', he wrote, 'comes *through* the Sacraments; is received *by* faith; *consists* in God's inward presence, and *lives* in obedience.' 'Whether we say we are justified by faith, or by works, or by Sacraments, all these but mean this one doctrine, that we are justified by grace, which is given through Sacraments, impetrated by faith, manifested in works.' [24]

But what saith the Scripture? Well, clearly the Scriptures define the divine method of the justification of the sinner in both negative and positive terms. Indeed, it is crucial that a doctrine as vulnerable to heresy as that of the divine method of the sinner's justification should be safeguarded by the use of both negative and positive terms. The negative statements are just as important as the positive statements for the Apostle Paul. 'Knowing', he writes to the Galatian Church, 'that a man is not justified by the works of the law, but by the faith of Jesus Christ, even we have believed in Jesus Christ, that we might be justified by the faith of Christ, and not by the works of the law: for by the works of the law shall no flesh be justified.' The Apostle Paul, with his remarkable emphases and repetition here, defines justification in terms of antithesis, and not in terms of synthesis. Justification by faith alone and justification by works are opposites, and cannot be reconciled. Any attempt, therefore to fuse justification by faith alone and justification by works, will inevitably result in the destruction of the system of justification by faith alone. There is no possible *via media* between these two positions; they are utterly incompatible and totally irreconcilable. G. S. Faber was right, therefore, to underline the logical absurdity of a position in which, according to Newman,

> we are justified by faith; we are justified by obedience; we are justified by baptism; we are justified conjointly by the two sacraments of baptism and the Lord's Supper. Our Justification precedes our faith, and our faith precedes our Justification. The word Justification cannot bear two meanings, yet it clearly does bear two meanings, to wit, the *accounting* righteous, and the *making* righteous. There is but one act of Justification, nevertheless there are ten thousand Justifications.

Faber was right to describe Newman's *Lectures* as 'a tissue of contradictions and inconsistencies'. For it is manifest that although Newman had an extremely subtle and ingenious mind, he did not have a very logical mind; there is this element of irrationality in Newman. Genius though he was in many respects, his avowed antipathy to logic is his Achilles' heel. 'Newman', writes Professor Owen Chadwick, 'dismissed theological logic.' 'He is always skimming', writes G. M. Young, 'along the verge of a logical catastrophe.' Now this antipathy to logic is one of the most significant features of the Romantic mind. David Newsome, in his fascinating book entitled *Two Classes of Men*, has shown that the Romantics seized upon 'the idea of the reconciliation of opposites as the universal law for which they were seeking'; 'the concept . . . of the reconciliation of opposites', Newsome asserts, 'is the key to a true understanding of Romantic philosophy'. The Romantics had this great urge 'to find the One behind the many'; they were preoccupied with the synthesizing of opposites, and this involved a fascination with paradox, and a toleration of contradiction. There can be no doubt, however, that when the Romantic mind applies itself in this way to the divine method of justification, there are very grave dangers involved. In his vain attempt to reconcile the irreconcilable, Newman is found guilty of perverting the

21

gospel of Christ and frustrating the grace of God. His gospel is 'another gospel, which is not another', and Dr James Bennett was not overstating his case when he contended that since the Council of Trent, 'perhaps there never has been a book published, at least among Protestants, more full of insidious, but determined, opposition to the Lord Jesus Christ as our righteousness. Contradiction, obscurity, mystification, . . .—all are brought into the field, to bear against the only righteousness in which a sinner can stand before God.'[25]

The Sacramental Principle

Inextricably related, of course, to their doctrine of justification was the Tractarians' great emphasis upon the 'sacramental principle'. For Tractarian theology was characterized by a deepening sacramentalism which again coalesced well with the Romantic spirit that was afloat, with its yearning for mystery, reverence, and awe; it coalesced well with the symbolic and sacramental consciousness of the Romantic mind. Newman, indeed, regarded this 'sacramental principle', or 'sacramental system', as one of the three pivotal fundamental features of the Oxford Movement, alongside the principle of dogma and, ironically, the principle of anti-Romanism. The Tractarian doctrine of the Church was that of 'a visible Church, with sacraments and rites which are the channels of invisible grace.' The Tractarians believed in 'sacramental justification'; they believed in 'baptismal regeneration'. For them, 'sacramental grace' was conferred automatically via participation in the sacraments. 'All those who have partaken of the ordinances of the Church', asserted the Tractarians, 'are born again'. The Tractarians emphasized, then, the inherent efficacy of the sacraments, and asserted that God has established an invariable connection between the observance of these external ordinances and the communication of spiritual blessings. In their doctrine of 'baptismal regeneration', for instance, they taught that all those that have been baptized are born again and have been made partakers of the divine nature. For Dr Pusey, the great Tractarian spokesman on this subject, baptism was itself 'the washing of regeneration', and involved both the remission of sins and the implantation of divine life into the soul. It is remarkable that some Evangelicals were not unhappy with this doctrine of baptismal regeneration. Others, however, realized at once that not only was such a doctrine heretical, but also that it constituted a massive and perilous stumbling-block in the way of the true regeneration of the sinner. Merle d'Aubigné, for instance, contended strongly that 'malice could not invent a stratagem more likely to impede conversion than this idea that all men baptized of water are regenerated'. 'The Puseyite system', he wrote, 'tends to lull consciences by participating in exterior rites; the evangelical system tends continually to awaken them.' There is, moreover, a very real contemporary relevance to this issue and to d'Aubigné's cogent comments upon this issue, in that at the time of the visit of Pope John-Paul II to these shores in 1982, the leading Anglican Evangelical, the Rev. John Stott, referred, in the course of an article published in *The Times* on the relationship between the Church of Rome and the Church of England, to 'our common baptismal faith.' Now it is extremely difficult to understand what an Evangelical can mean by such a phrase when one considers that the Roman Catholic Church, for its part, teaches quite unashamedly a doctrine of baptismal regeneration. It is surely high time to assert categorically that for an Evangelical to hold to the doctrine of baptismal regeneration is a total contradiction in terms, and involves not only considerable confusion of thought, but also a radical undermining of the very foundations of the Protestant Evangelical faith. [26]

With regard to the sacrament of the Lord's Supper, the Tractarians taught the doctrine of the Real Presence or Consubstantiation. Pusey was again their chief spokesman in this, and his doctrine was this: that in the Lord's Supper the bread and the wine are so influenced and operated on by the act of consecration, that although bread and wine remain, yet there is by consecration a real, though spiritual and supernatural presence of the body and blood of Christ which are so united to the bread and wine as to form with them one compound whole. Now clearly this doctrine of Consubstantiation avoids some of the grosser absurdities of the Roman Catholic doctrine of Transubstantiation, and yet it is, like the doctrine of baptismal regeneration, rooted and grounded in the *ex opere operato* principle of Rome itself. Both doctrines impute a mechanical, mechanistic, even magical efficacy to the sacraments, and are most dangerous precisely because of the natural tendencies of the human heart. 'If these doctrines prevail in the Church', d'Aubigné contended, 'Christianity will cease to be a new life, a holy life, a spiritual life, a heavenly life. It will become an affair of exterior ordinances, rites and ceremonies.' Again, Dr William Cunningham—a man who always emphasized that it was a great mistake to underrate the strength and subtlety of Romish theology—made the following cogent and incisive statement with regard to the 'sacramental principle' of the Oxford Movement:

> If popery be Satan's masterpiece, the theory and practice of the sacraments may perhaps be regarded as the most finished and perfect department in this great work of his. And it is not in the least surprising, that when recently the great adversary set himself to check and overturn the scriptural and evangelical principles which were gaining a considerable influence in the Church of England, he should have chiefly made use of the sacramental principle for effecting his design,—that is, the principle that there is an invariable connection between participation in the sacraments and the enjoyment of spiritual blessings, and that the sacraments have an inherent power or virtue whereby they produce these appropriate effects. In no other way, and by no other process, could he have succeeded to such an extent as he has done, in leading men to disregard and despise all that Scripture teaches us concerning our helpless and ruined condition by nature; concerning the necessity of a regeneration of our moral nature by the power of the Holy Spirit; concerning the way and manner in which, according to the divine method of

justification, pardon and acceptance have been procured and are bestowed; concerning the place and function of faith in the salvation of sinners, and concerning the true elements and distinguishing characteristics of all those things that accompany salvation, —and, finally, in no other way could he have succeeded to such an extent in leading men who have been ministers in a Protestant church to submit openly and unreservedly to that system of doctrine and practice which is immeasurably better fitted than any other to accomplish his purposes, by leading men to build wholly upon a false foundation, and to reject the counsel of God against themselves; while it is better fitted than any other to retain men in the most degrading, and, humanly speaking, the most hopeless bondage.

For without ever formally denying the message of the Cross, the 'sacramental principle' tends by its very nature to throw the Cross of Christ into the background and thus to neutralize its efficacy and power. It is this 'sacramental principle' which constitutes the masterpiece within the masterpiece of Satan. [27]

Attitudes to the Reformation

Clearly, then, the Oxford Movement, with its 'sacramental principle', its doctrine of justification, and its excessive deference to the Fathers, involved a definite antagonism to the great principles of the Protestant Reformation, for it involved the attempted overthrow, by men within the Church of England, of those hallmarks of the Protestant faith—the *sola scriptura* principle, the *sola gratia* principle, and the principle of *sola fide*. Indeed, Tractarianism demonstrated itself increasingly to be anti-Scriptural, anti-Evangelical, and anti-Protestant; and if some Evangelicals were slow to realize or acknowledge this, then all remaining doubts on this score should have been removed by the publication in 1838 of the literary *Remains* of Newman's great friend, the deceased Richard Hurrell Froude. 'Really I hate the Reformation and the Reformers more and more', Froude had written. 'The Reformation was a limb badly set—it must be broken again

25

in order to be righted.' Froude, a great admirer of medieval Catholicism, asserted that the Tractarian position was this: 'We are Catholics without Popery, and Church of England men without Protestantism.' Thus, whilst it was true that, in the early stages at least, one of the avowed aims of the Oxford Movement was the principle of anti-Romanism, in actual fact the spirit of anti-Protestantism was a much more prominent feature of the Movement, and this inevitably so, since Catholic principles and Catholic dogma are infinitely more anti-Protestant than anti-Romanist. There was this common desire amongst the Tractarians to undo the Reformation of the sixteenth century and to 'unprotestantize the national Church'. Newman himself spoke of the need for 'a second Reformation:—a better reformation, for it would be a return not to the sixteenth century, but to the seventeenth'. It was a return to the theology of the Caroline divines and the Non-jurors of the seventeenth century that Newman desired—a return to the High Church tradition of men such as Andrewes, Hammond and Laud. It is not in the least surprising, therefore, that the Tractarians began to manifest an increasing indulgence to Rome, and indeed an increasing nostalgia for Rome. 'Speak *gently* of thy sister's fall,' John Keble had urged in his *Christian Year*. Again, Hurrell Froude's dying exhortation against uncharitableness with regard to Rome had its impact upon Newman. 'I learned', wrote Newman, 'to have tender feelings towards her'; and by 1840 he had himself drawn up prayers for Christian unity. There was increasingly in John Henry Newman this same irenic, quasi-ecumenical spirit, and it is surely not at all without significance that the seeds of the Ecumenical Movement were sown in this poetic, Romantic and sentimental climate of the Oxford Movement. It was in this climate that Christian love was elevated above Christian truth, and Christian truth was sacrificed to Christian unity; it was in this climate that men began to 'put darkness for light, and light for darkness', and held up the great and glorious Protestant Reformation of the sixteenth century as the great scapegoat of the Christian Church. It must never be forgotten, therefore, that the Movement of 1833 which some historians hail as the 'Anglican Revival' of the nineteenth century was in fact essentially an Oxford Counter-Reformation. [28]

Tract 90

As far as the Tractarians themselves were concerned, however, it was initially a *via media* or middle system that they sought to establish. This concept of the *via media* or 'golden mean' was, of course, by no means new or original in the Church of England; Mathew Parker, the first Elizabethan archbishop of Canterbury in the sixteenth century, had spoken of this 'golden mean' which would, he felt, preserve within the fold of the one Church both Protestants and Catholics. John Henry Newman, however, felt that the *via media* needed to be defined more closely—he wanted to draw it out into a definite shape and character. 'It was not as yet objective and real', he wrote. 'It was at present a paper religion.' Newman wanted to buttress and fortify this middle system; he wanted to prove that Anglo-Catholicism was in fact a 'substantive religion'. It was, then, with this intention in mind that Newman published, in February 1841, Tract 90, the last and most famous of the Tracts, on the subject of the 39 Articles. Essentially Tract 90 was, for Newman, an experiment—'a hazardous experiment,—like proving cannon', he said. He wanted to make 'fair trial how much the English Church will bear', to inquire 'how far the Articles were tolerant of a Catholic, or even a Roman interpretation'. Newman wanted to see how great an infusion of Catholic truth the Church of England would bear before it burst, as it were, only to show that she was after all purely and essentially Protestant. It was his contention that the 39 Articles were 'ambiguous formularies', that they were characterized by 'vagueness and indecisiveness', that there was an 'elasticity' about them, and that they were therefore 'not uncatholic'. The first principle of all in Tract 90, Newman asserted, was 'to take our reformed confessions in the most Catholic sense they will admit: we have no duties towards their framers'. [29]

Newman's 'hazardous experiment', however, failed. Tract 90 met with considerable opposition, and justifiably so, for there can be no doubt that Newman was overstating his case with regard to the alleged Catholic sense of the 39 Articles. Evangelical Protestants are not afraid to concede, however, that Newman's case does have a certain plausibility, for it is undeniable that the 39 Articles did provide Newman with a lever and a handle for his position. It is undeniable that there are weaknesses and deficiencies in the 39 Articles which can be exploited by anyone who is bent on making the Articles, rather than the Holy Scriptures, the judge and arbiter of truth. It cannot be denied, for instance, that Article 27 is a very unsatisfactory statement on the subject of baptism and leaves the door open for a doctrine of baptismal regeneration when it asserts that 'Baptism is not only a sign of profession and mark of difference . . . but is also a sign of regeneration or new birth whereby, as by an instrument, they that receive Baptism rightly are grafted into the Church'. There is a confusion here between baptism as a sign of regeneration, and baptism as an instrument of regeneration, so that John Henry Newman would be quite entitled, in this case, to assert the 'vagueness and indecisiveness', indeed the 'elasticity', of this particular Article. Article 27 is indeed, in this respect, an 'ambiguous formulary'. Again, it cannot be denied that Article 28, on the subject of the Lord's Supper, gives the Tractarians a lever and a handle for their doctrine of the Real Presence; for whilst the doctrine of Transubstantiation is rejected as 'repugnant to the plain words of Scripture', the door is left open for a doctrine of Consubstantiation to be construed from the following statement: 'The body of Christ is given, taken, and eaten, in the Supper, only after an heavenly and spiritual manner.' These are words which harmonize well with Pusey's insistence upon a real, though spiritual and supernatural, presence of the body of Christ in the Lord's Supper, and may in that sense be described in Newman's words as 'not uncatholic'. Again, it cannot be denied that Articles 32 and 36 contain some dangerous statements on the subject of 'Priests'; for in

28

these two Articles 'Priests' are tacitly accepted as part of the Anglican doctrine of the 'three orders' of 'Bishops, Priests, and Deacons'. Once again, it cannot be denied that the Church of England has never rid itself of the concept of a special priesthood; there is a Catholic undertone within the 39 Articles.[30]

However, it must be pointed out in response to Newman that the real issue with regard to the 39 Articles is not in fact the degree of their 'catholicity', but rather the degree of their scripturalness. The great question with regard to the Articles should not be how far the Articles are tolerant of a Catholic interpretation, but rather how far the Articles reflect faithfully the doctrine of God's Holy Word. The great tragedy of John Henry Newman lies in his over-preoccupation, indeed his obsession, with the Creeds and Articles of men. It must never be forgotten that the latter are not infallible, and indeed that they are characterized by real inadequacies and deficiencies, and must themselves be ever brought to the bar of the infallible Word of God. It is the Scriptures—not the Articles—which 'cannot be broken'.[31]

For Newman, however, the opposition and hostility aroused by Tract 90 meant the demolition of the *via media* as a definite theory. Moreover, this collapse of the *via media* theory was hastened in Newman's mind by his study of the Arian controversy in the summer of 1841. Newman saw that in the Arian controversy there were three parties—the pure Arians, the semi-Arians, and Rome. The pure Arians, he contended, were the heretics; the semi-Arians represented the *via media* position; whilst the truth in the Arian controversy lay with the Church of Rome. Similarly in the nineteenth century, Newman asserted, Protestants are the heretics; Anglicans represent the *via media* position; whilst the truth lies with Rome. 'The truth lay, not with the *Via Media*,' Newman wrote, 'but with what was called "the extreme party".' 'In the controversies of the early centuries', Newman contended, 'the Roman Church was ever on the right side, which was of course a *prima facie* argument in favour of Rome and against Anglicanism now.' Newman's reasoning here is, of course, a classic *non sequitur*. It is a prime example of the danger of that reasoning by analogy in which he so delighted. It simply does not follow that, because the Church of Rome was on the side of truth in the Arian controversy and in certain other controversies of the early centuries, she is necessarily on the side of truth in all other doctrines. Evangelical Protestants are ready to concede that the Church of Rome is orthodox in its doctrine of the Person of Christ and of the Trinity, just as they are ready to assert that the Church of Rome is heretical in its doctrine of the sacraments and of the justification of the sinner. Darkness and light are mixed together in the Church of Rome, and damnable heresies coexist together with certain truths. Questions of doctrine, therefore, are not settled *en bloc* by means of subtle, historical parallels; rather they are settled by bringing them, one by one, to the scrutiny of the Holy Word of God. Newman, however, had come by this route to the conclusion that the *via media* was 'untenable', that it was 'an impossible idea', that it was in fact merely 'a paper system', and that the Church of England was merely a 'paper Church'. By the end of 1841 Newman was on his 'death-bed' with regard to his membership of the Anglican Church. [32]

Evangelical Reaction

Meanwhile, since the commencement of the Oxford Movement in 1833, Evangelical reaction to Tractarianism had been gathering momentum. Initially, however, there was a certain sluggishness, even a certain confusion, in the response of Evangelicals to the Movement. In the early days of the Movement, Evangelical suspicion of the Tractarians was mixed with Evangelical co-operation with the Tractarians. Peter Toon, for instance, notes that within Anglican Evangelicalism in 1834 'there were those Evangelicals who were, to say the least, sympathetic to its seemingly spiritual character'. Thus during the first few years of the Movement there was a critical delay in any serious controversy between Anglican Evangelicals and Tractarians. David Newsome, for his part, in his book *The Parting of Friends*, has shown that

30

Gladstone was wrong in his assertion that the Evangelicals 'joined . . . in utterly condemning the Tractarian movement from the first'. Indeed Newsome asserts that 'in many ways the Tractarians appeared—in the early stages of the Oxford Movement—to be the continuators of the Evangelicals'; and Professor Owen Chadwick substantiates this idea when he writes: 'there is a certain continuity of piety between the Evangelical movement and the Oxford Movement . . . . Both Newman and Pusey brought into the movement a strong element of Evangelical sensibility and language.' The writings of the Tractarians do indeed reveal a great insistence upon holiness, upon the loathsomeness of sin, upon the narrowness of the way, upon the vanity of this world, upon self-denial, upon unworldliness and other-worldliness, upon eternal realities 'beyond the veil', upon the presence of Christ and of God. There can be no doubt but that these emphases provided a quasi-Evangelical note to Tractarian teaching. However, if there was this apparent 'continuity of piety' between Evangelicalism and Tractarianism, it became increasingly evident that there was not, in certain crucial areas, a continuity of doctrine. The Tractarian Rule of Faith, the Tractarian doctrine of justification, the 'sacramental principle' and the Tractarian doctrine of 'Reserve'—these were the areas which proved before long that there was a great gulf fixed between the Catholic sacramentalism of the Oxford Movement on the one hand and Evangelical theology on the other; and if certain Anglican Evangelicals were rather slow to recognize the dangers of Tractarianism, then this must to some extent be attributed to the Catholic undertone inherent in the formularies of Anglicanism itself.[33]

However, if there was something of a lull before the storm, eventually the storm did break in 1837-8, and it involved a national outcry against Tractarianism. Peter Toon, in his recent work entitled *Evangelical Theology 1833-1856: A Response to Tractarianism*, indicates that there was a tremendous output of Evangelical literature in response to the Oxford Movement. 'There was certainly quantity, if not quality, in the mass of material', Toon asserts. Considerable quality was, however, evident in the writings of the most learned and able of the Anglican Evangelicals who responded to Tractarianism, namely William Goode, whose scholarly writings were warmly commended by the great Scottish theologian, Dr William Cunningham. As for the Anglican periodicals, the editor of the *Christian Lady's Magazine* described Tractarianism as an 'approximation to Popery', whilst the *Christian Observer* spoke of 'the character and evils of the system inculcated in the Oxford Tracts; which even weeping, we believe to be anti-Evangelical, anti-Protestant', 'Popery in disguise'. [34]

Again, an excellent critique of the Oxford Movement was produced by Dr Merle d'Aubigné in the lecture which he delivered at the opening meeting of the Theological School of Geneva in 1842. In this lecture d'Aubigné argued that there had been three distinct epochs in the Church prior to the Reformation—that of 'Evangelical Christianity' in the first and second centuries of the Church, where authority is attributed to the revealed Word of God, and where it is God who reigns; that of 'Ecclesiastical Catholicism', from the third to the seventh centuries, where authority is attributed to the Church, and where it is man who reigns; and that of the 'Roman Papacy', from the seventh to the fifteenth centuries, where authority is attributed to the Pope, and where it is Antichrist who reigns. The Oxford Movement, d'Aubigné contended, was a 'new system of ecclesiastical catholicism'. It was 'a human and sacerdotal religion' which, whilst formally rejecting popery, 'nearly approaches popery, for it already contains the germ of all the principles found there'. D'Aubigné warned that the Church of England stood 'on the edge of the abyss'. 'The Tiber flows in Oxford', he asserted. 'Oxford conducts to Rome.' [35]

Precisely the same note was struck by Professor James Garbett in his Bampton Lectures of 1842. 'The system', he contended,

> is Romanism; not partially, but essentially; not *yet* Romanism, indeed, as historical recollections have

32

expressed it, or as the conclusions of reason have demonstrated it to be; not Romanism in *all* its palpable and revolting incongruities to the heart and understanding. But—Romanism, as it has, in all ages, represented itself to the young and to the devout—Romanism, as it is when purified by elevated feelings, and minds originally trained in Scripture truth—Romanism, as it combines with itself all that is grand and beautiful in art, specious in reason and seductive in sentiment—Romanism, which may be safe in those scripturally-trained minds who have presented it to themselves and to the world in this beautified shape—but Romanism, still perverting the truth of the Gospel while it decorates it—Romanism, which though it looks paternally and benignly in the amiable spirits of its present advocates, involves principles ever fatal to human liberty and progression—Romanism, with the establishment of whose theory the Articles of the Church of England cannot coexist, and whose unseen and unavowed operations in *practice* will paralyse her spiritual power and destroy the Church of Christ, by substituting human forms for her Prophet, Priest and King. [36]

Newman's Secession to Rome

Moreover, the actual secession of John Henry Newman to the Church of Rome itself in 1845, together with a large number of his friends, may be fairly said to have settled the question of the general tendency of Tractarian or Anglo-Catholic views. 'Romanism', commented William Cunningham,

> is the legitimate development of Tractarianism . . . . Tractarianism substantially agrees with Romanism in corrupting, and in the way in which it corrupts, the rule of faith, the divine method of justification, and the whole worship and government of the Church of Christ. Their agreement upon these points is great and substantial, while their differences are trifling and incidental.

'It was very manifest all along', Cunningham remarked,

that while the Tractarians expressed disapprobation of some of the particular tenets and practices of the Romanists, they had really, though probably to some extent unconsciously, embraced the whole substance, all the guiding and fundamental principles, of Popery, almost everything about it that makes it injurious to the souls of men, and ruinous to the interests of true religion.

In this same article Cunningham maintained that no event of a similar nature had taken place in any Protestant Church since the Reformation, and that whilst individual instances of the apostasy of Protestant ministers to the Church of Rome had occurred in almost all the Reformed Churches, never before had this apostasy been exhibited on so large a scale. It was for this reason, Cunningham rightly contended, that the secession of Newman and of a large number of his friends, was 'well fitted to arrest attention, and to afford useful lessons and solemn warnings to the Churches of Christ'.[37]

Particularly instructive are the reasons given by Newman for his joining the Church of Rome. 'My one paramount reason', he wrote, 'for contemplating a change is my deep, unvarying conviction that our Church is in schism, and that my salvation depends on my joining the Church of Rome.' 'The simple question is, Can *I* (it is personal, not whether another, but can *I*) be saved in the English Church? Am *I* in safety, were I to die tonight? Is it a mortal sin in *me*, not joining another communion?' Rome had by now cast its spell over John Henry Newman, and it was a spell that bewitched and beguiled this tragic genius, with his towering intellect, into the clutches of her bondage—a spell in which spiritual fear was mingled with Romantic attraction. Thus in John Henry Newman we see the workings of the Catholic mind, with its great emphasis upon the visible Church and upon the visible unity of the Church, with its great fear of lying outside of Rome, with its conviction that salvation depends upon the Church, and with its readiness to be greatly impressed and overawed by the massive historical phenomenon of Rome. 'My mind fell back upon itself in relaxation and in peace,' wrote Newman after joining Rome, 'and I gazed at her almost passively as a great objective fact. I looked at her;—at her rites, her ceremonial, and her precepts; and I said "This *is* a religion"'; and then, when I looked back upon the poor Anglican Church, for which I had laboured so hard, and upon all that appertained to it, and thought of our various attempts to dress it up doctrinally and aesthetically, it seemed to me to be the veriest of nonentities'—'a mere national institution'.[38]

Moreover, the secession of John Henry Newman and of a large number of his friends served to refute the delusion that the extension of education and the spread of secular knowledge afforded of themselves an adequate safeguard and security against the extension of Romanism. William Cunningham contended that this was one of the major lessons to emerge from the Oxford Movement, namely that

> the mere diffusion of education and of general knowledge, does not, of itself, afford any adequate security against the revival and extension of Romanism. Many have been accustomed to cherish the notion that, in the midst of the light and liberty of the nineteenth century, it was quite chimerical to apprehend that Popery, with all its fooleries and absurdities, could ever again acquire any influence over the minds of men. But we have seen a system which is in substance Popery, and includes a great deal of what is usually reckoned most irrational and absurd in the tenets and practices of the Church of Rome, spread with marvellous rapidity among the most highly educated youth of our country.

Evangelicals today must, therefore, never forget, nor ever underestimate 'the natural Popery of the human heart'.[39]

Romantic Aesthetics

In this context, moreover, it must not be forgotten that a significant factor in the phenomenal growth of the Oxford Movement was the establishment in 1839 of a complementary movement in Cambridge—the Cambridge Camden Society, committed to the 'study of Gothic Architecture and Ritual

Arts'. Romantic aesthetics ruled the day, and these Romantic aesthetics greatly favoured the Gothic, and the Gothic in turn led men back to the medievalism of the fourteenth century and to inevitable connotations of Roman Catholicism. The Camdenians felt that medieval churches possessed inner, mystical meaning; they felt that architecture possessed not only an artistic significance, but also a spiritual significance. Indeed, the Camdenians advised the modern architects of the day to make exact copies of medieval churches; they believed, writes Professor Owen Chadwick, that 'Gothic was the only Christian style of architecture'. [40]

Now, this new concern for beauty in architecture was again part of the Romantic spirit of the age. Professor Owen Chadwick writes, for instance, of 'the sense of affection and the sensibility of beauty pervading European thought'. There was a desire afloat 'to make the churches numinous, to transform them from bare houses of preaching into temples evocative of prayer'. There was this new 'quest for reverence' in architecture, the feeling that churches should be made more like cathedrals, a concern more for the atmosphere of worship than the preaching of the Word of God. Thus the spirit of Romanticism produced a very dangerous confusion between the artistic or aesthetic on the one hand, and the spiritual on the other hand. Back in the year 1820, for instance, the poet John Keats had written these famous words in his 'Ode on a Grecian Urn':

> *'Beauty is truth, truth beauty'—that is all*
> *Ye know on earth, and all ye need to know.*

Keats here is asserting not only the beauty of truth, but also the truth of beauty. He is suggesting not only the beauty of holiness, but also the holiness of beauty; and it is this latter idea of the truth or holiness of beauty—the naive, romantic, and unbiblical assumption that the beautiful is necessarily true and holy—which constituted such a powerful and dangerous idea in the hands of the Camdenians and subsequently the Ritualists as they moved unerringly and inevitably in the direction of Rome. [41]

Thus in practice the Camdenians wanted to alter the internal arrangements of most Anglican churches where hitherto the pulpit had been dominant. They introduced sanctuaries, altars and crosses; they introduced statues, candlesticks, choirs in surplices, and stained glass windows. There was this flowering of Victorian Gothic architecture, and it coalesced very easily with the deepening Catholic sacramentalism of Oxford. Indeed, the 'symbolical principle' of Cambridge developed naturally and almost inevitably out of the 'sacramental principle' of Oxford. Thus Francis Close of Cheltenham, preaching on Guy Fawkes Day 1844, contended that 'as Romanism is taught *Analytically* at Oxford, it is taught *Artistically* at Cambridge . . . . It is inculcated theoretically in Tracts at the one University and it is *sculptured, painted* and *graven* at the other'. It was in this way that theology and architecture acted and reacted upon one another, and mutually reinforced each other, producing an utterly unscriptural ritualism and sacerdotalism. Merle d'Aubigné's remarkable prophecy in his lecture of 1842 had been realized:

> If they put the Church above Christianity, form above life, they shall infallibly reap that which they have sown, they shall soon have for a church, an assembly of skeletons, brilliantly clothed perhaps; ranged, I grant, in admirable order, imposing to the flesh; but icy, motionless, and resembling a pale legion of the dead. If Puseyism . . . advance in the English Church, in a few years the sources of her life will be dried. The feverish excitement which the malady at first produced, will soon give place to languor, the blood will congeal, the muscles will freeze, and that Church shall soon be no more than a dead body, upon which the eagles shall come from all quarters to feed.

It was indeed not long before the quasi-Evangelical note had disappeared from Anglo-Catholicism, and the smouldering fires of Tractarianism developed increasingly into what J. C. Ryle was to describe as a 'sensuous, histrionic, formal religion'; it was the living death of an extreme Ritualism.

Again, with the Lux Mundi movement of 1889, the second and third generation of Tractarians, led by Charles Gore, welded Liberalism to Catholicism, producing the double evil of a liberal sacramentalism which has become such a dominant force in world Anglicanism in the twentieth century.[42]

Trends in Contemporary Evangelicalism

As we turn now to the contemporary situation in Evangelicalism today, we find that there is a very real relevance to the issues involved in the Oxford Movement of 150 years ago. The last 16 years or so, for instance, have witnessed a quite astonishing *rapprochement* between Anglican Evangelicals and Anglo-Catholics. The tone for this new atmosphere of *détente* was set at the Keele Congress of 1967, when Anglican Evangelicals issued this statement:

> Polemics at long range have at times in the past led us into negative and impoverishing 'anti'-attitudes (anti-sacramental, anti-intellectual, etc.) from which we now desire to shake free. We recognise that in dialogue we may hope to learn truths held by others to which we have hitherto been blind, as well as to impart to others truths held by us and overlooked by them.

Since Keele in 1967 there has been this new commitment on the part of Evangelicals in the Church of England to 'dialogue' and 'encounter' with Anglo-Catholics, the heirs of the Oxford Movement itself. Moreover, three years later, in 1970, the first major fruit of this new relationship was published—*Growing into Union: Proposals for forming a united Church in England*—a work that was issued jointly by two Anglo-Catholics, the Rev. Prof. Eric L. Mascall and Dr Graham Leonard (then Bishop of Willesden, now of London), and two Evangelicals, the Rev. Colin Buchanan and Dr James Packer. At the very outset of this work we find quoted with approval the following statement made by Dr A. M. Ramsey, the future Archbishop of Canterbury, in 1956:

'Catholicism' and 'Evangelicalism' are not two separate things which the Church of England must hold together by a great feat of compromise. Rightly understood, they are both facts which lie behind the Church of England and, as the New Testament shows, they are one fact. A church's witness to the one Church of the ages is a part of its witness to the Gospel of God.

Now this is a quite astonishing assertion—it is quite breathtaking in its cavalier adventurism! For whilst it is quite true that 'Catholicism' and 'Evangelicalism' are 'both facts which lie behind the Church of England', it is surely only a fevered Romantic imagination that can assert that 'they are one fact'. For this bland assertion that 'they are one fact' is surely a classic example of that spirit of Romanticism which ever yearns for the synthesizing and the reconciliation of opposites and which ever aspires to 'find the One behind the many'. Moreover, the bland assertion, quoted with approval by two leading Anglican Evangelicals, that 'the New Testament shows' that 'they are one fact' is a statement which is so palpably untrue that it deserves no ordinary severity of castigation.[43]

It is interesting, however, to notice the extent to which the shadow of John Henry Newman lies across the pages of *Growing into Union*. Very early in the first chapter, entitled 'Scripture and Tradition', Newman is mentioned as the figure who, to all intents and purposes, was the first to introduce a theory of the development of Christian doctrine. This he wrote in 1845 to justify in his own mind his own imminent secession to the Church of Rome. Now the originality of Newman's famous essay lay in his assertion that truth is to be regarded as dynamic, and not static, in quality. Christian doctrine, Newman contended, was something that developed —it had this organic and dynamic quality—it was something that evolved. 'Christian doctrine', he wrote, 'admits of formal, legitimate, and true developments, that is, of developments contemplated by its Divine Author.' 'Modern Catholicism', asserted Newman, 'is nothing else but simply the legitimate growth and complement, that is the natural and necessary development, of the doctrine of the early church, and . . . its divine authority is included in the divinity of Christianity'. Thus when, in the context of John Henry Newman, the authors of *Growing into Union* contend that 'there can be and is development in the Church's understanding of the Gospel', they are not making a harmless statement about a development in the Church's *subjective* understanding of the Gospel once delivered unto the saints; with a certain sleight of hand they are asserting that there has been, down through the centuries, an *objective* development of Christian doctrine itself. They speak approvingly of 'the recovery of a dynamic view of Tradition as essentially the process of the handing on by the Church of the faith of the Scriptures'. Astonishingly, both Buchanan and Packer are giving an unqualified endorsement of the aforementioned position of John Henry Newman.[44]

Evangelical Protestants are, therefore, entitled to ask Buchanan and Packer whether this endorsement of Newman's theory of the development of Christian doctrine also includes the following breathtaking assertion on Newman's part:

> The Incarnation is the antecedent of the doctrine of Mediation, and the archetype both of the Sacramental principle and of the merits of Saints. From the doctrine of Mediation follow the Atonement, the Mass, the merits of Martyrs and Saints, their invocation and *cultus*. From the Sacramental principle come the Sacraments properly so called; the unity of the Church, and the Holy See as its type and centre; the authority of Councils; the sanctity of rites; the veneration of holy places, shrines, images, vessels, furniture, and vestments. Of the Sacraments, Baptism is developed into Confirmation on the one hand; into Penance, Purgatory, and Indulgences on the other; and the Eucharist into the Real Presence, adoration of the Host, Resurrection of the body, and the virtue of relics. Again, the doctrine of the Sacraments leads to the doctrine of Justification; Justification to that of Original Sin; Original Sin to the merit of Celibacy.[45]

Is *this* what Buchanan and Packer mean when they say that 'there can be and is development in the Church's understanding of the Gospel'? For such is Newman's dynamic view of Tradition in actual practice and such is the thorough recklessness with which he applies it. William Cunningham's comment on Newman's theory is, therefore, most relevant today:

> It seems to us, that the man who, after due investigation, has persuaded himself that the system of doctrine, government, and worship, held in the modern Church of Rome, is a legitimate development, and not a corruption, of apostolic Christianity, should be willing and ready to maintain, that the polytheism and idolatry of the ancient heathen world was a development and not a corruption of the patriarchal religion, and that the pharisaic system of our Saviour's days was a development and not a corruption of the religion which God communicated to the Jews through Moses.[46]

Protestants, Cunningham rightly maintained, are the defenders of the theory of a corruption in Christian doctrine, and contend that the modern Church of Rome is the ultimate product of such a corruption.

Again, the third chapter in *Growing into Union*, entitled 'Church and Sacraments', reveals a quite lamentable capitulation by Buchanan and Packer to the 'sacramental principle' of Anglo-Catholicism with its great emphasis upon the efficacy of the sacraments. 'The language of Scripture about them', asserts *Growing into Union*,

> is the language of sheer unqualified efficacy. If the outward celebration is performed, then on the first showing the inward grace is mediated. Those who have been baptized into Christ 'have put on Christ' . . . . Those who receive communion receive the body and blood of Christ . . . . The simple expectation is that those who partake of the sacraments are partakers in them and by them of God's grace . . . . The overall picture is one of serene objectivity and confidence on the writers' part in the efficacy of the sacraments.[47]

Now this is surely as bold an assertion of 'sacramental grace' as any Anglo-Catholic could desire, and it is both astonishing and highly regrettable that two leading Anglican Evangelicals should be signatories to such a statement which inevitably involves a radical undermining of the great Evangelical and Protestant doctrines of regeneration by the sovereign Spirit of God and of justification by faith alone in the merits of Jesus Christ. It is but a further lamentable proof of the grave dangers which confront Evangelicals who are prepared to engage in ecumenical 'dialogue' and 'encounter'.

Moreover, when we turn to *The Final Report* of the Anglican-Roman Catholic International Commission, published in 1982, we observe again the capitulation of the lone Evangelical voice of the Rev. Julian Charley to the Catholic cast of thought which clearly dominates the Commission. Once again the shadow of John Henry Newman lies across the pages of the Report; once again we find an implicit endorsement of Newman's theory of the development of Christian doctrine in the following reference to Tradition as 'the growth of the seed of God's word from age to age'. We are assured, however, by *The Final Report* that this approach 'does not necessarily contradict' the *sola scriptura* approach of never going beyond the bounds of Scripture. To this we reply that the concept of the historical development of the seed of God's word certainly does, as a mere theory, deny the sufficiency of the original revelation in the Scriptures, whilst in practice, as applied to the Church of Rome, it contradicts the content of that original revelation in the Scriptures. It would appear that Julian Charley and his fellow delegates in the Commission have imbibed Newman's Romantic antipathy to theological logic as they strain every muscle to reconcile the irreconcilable.[48]

With regard to *The Final Report*'s statements on Papal supremacy or 'universal primacy', the same note of capitulation and concession is evident. The Evangelical Anglican delegate is apparently quite happy with the following statement on the see of Rome: 'It seems appropriate that in any future union a universal primacy such

42

as has been described should be held by that see'; and with regard to the notion of the 'divine right' of the papacy, the same delegate is a signatory to the following statement: 'If it is understood as affirming that the universal primacy of the bishop of Rome is part of God's design for the universal *koinonia* then it need not be a matter of disagreement.' And yet despite Evangelical objections to this statement, Julian Charley assures us in his Grove booklet entitled *Rome, Canterbury, and the Future* that such statements are 'compatible with Scripture'. We reply that whilst such statements may be compatible with Newman's theory of development, they are certainly not compatible with Scripture.[49]

Again, in the Statement on Eucharistic Doctrine of 1971, the following assertion is made by the Commission: 'In the eucharistic prayer the church continues to make a perpetual memorial of Christ's death, and his members . . . enter into the movement of his self-offering'. Now there is a vagueness, an indecisiveness about this statement; it is an ambiguous formulary, and the spirit of John Henry Newman hovers over it. Indeed it is most significant that Julian Charley himself, in *Rome, Canterbury, and the Future*, specifically defends and specifically advocates the use of Newman's concept of 'the "elasticity" of dogma'. Since Vatican II, Julian Charley asserts, there has been this new vogue in 'elasticity'. 'Possibly', he writes, 'it is in the *Final Report* of ARCIC in 1982 that this "elasticity" is most evident', and Julian Charley goes on to commend the concept of 'the "elasticity" of what once seemed wholly unchangeable . . . . It is especially necessary', he contends, 'now that ecumenism has come into its own.' Thus according to Julian Charley, 'dogmas . . . possess an elasticity that had not hitherto been appreciated; . . . they can sometimes be stretched to the point when they are barely recognizable for what they were previously thought to be'. 'They have been shown capable of being re-expressed in a way that alters their whole perspective.' Thus whilst Julian Charley himself insists that 'firm theological foundations are essential to every

43

ecumenical enterprise', he in fact believes that these foundations should be made essentially of *elastic* so that they can incorporate not only Evangelicals, but also Anglo-Catholics and the Church of Rome itself! [50]

Again, on a somewhat different level, it is interesting to notice the reaction of the Rev. John Stott and the Bishop of Thetford, Timothy Dudley-Smith, to *The Final Report*. Writing in June 1982 as the co-chairmen of the Church of England Evangelical Council, they put forward some very valid questions to the authors of *The Final Report* on the subjects of Justification, the Eucharist, Priesthood, Authority, Tradition, the Marian dogmas and the Primacy of the Pope. Indeed, so valid are their questions on these vital, central issues that we find it very difficult to understand how they can also assert with regard to the Report that 'there is much in it to applaud'. Again, we find it very difficult to understand how two Evangelicals, with such crucial questions in their minds, can cheerfully assert the following as their opening remark: 'We write in the warm afterglow of the Pope's visit to Britain.' But above all, we find it almost incredible, as an exercise in sheer logic, how these co-chairmen can maintain that 'there is nothing inconsistent about affirming the Pope as a Christian leader, while at the same time asking questions about the claims of the papacy and the dogmas of the Roman Catholic Church'. On the contrary, we reply, there *is* something highly inconsistent about affirming the Pope as a Christian leader, while at the same time asking such fundamental questions about the claims of the papacy and the dogmas of the Roman Catholic Church. After all, Christian leadership is not just a matter of personal charisma. There is a great *sine qua non* about Christian leadership, and that is the possession of Christian truth—and that in the very areas in which Stott and Dudley-Smith are themselves now putting such relevant and crucial questions to Julian Charley and his fellow delegates. [51]

It is, again, most significant that the 150th anniversary of the Oxford Movement has been marked by the publication, under the editorship of the Rev. Colin Buchanan, of a Grove booklet entitled *Anglo-Catholic Worship: An Evangelical Appreciation after 150 years.* Buchanan himself describes this collection of brief articles as 'our birthday present to the heirs of the Oxford Movement'. 'We are deeply respectful of the catholic tradition in the Church of England', he writes. Moreover, he goes on to indicate the grounds for this *rapprochement* of Evangelicals and Catholics. 'Liberalism', writes Buchanan, 'has often united evangelicals and anglo-catholics in defending the same ground, whilst . . . the Charismatic Movement . . . has often united them in sharing the same experience'. Similarly, in April of 1983 a spokesman at the Loughborough Conference for Anglo-Catholics emphasized what Anglo-Catholics and Evangelicals hold in common, namely 'our very real commitment to positive, supernatural, biblical beliefs'. At the same conference Bishop Eric Kemp asserted that there was now 'nine-tenths of agreement' between the two groupings. He also predicted much closer links between Anglo-Catholics and Evangelicals, and suggested the possibility of a joint conference in five years time. Clearly, then, the great tendency amongst certain Evangelicals in recent years has been to maximize areas of common ground, and to minimize crucial areas of difference. However, we must ask such Evangelicals whether a common opposition to Liberalism, coupled with a common concern for spiritual experience and holiness, is a sufficient reason for such a *rapprochement*. After all, Evangelicals of a former generation acknowledged that they were constantly fighting a battle on two fronts— against liberal theology on the one front and against sacramental theology on the other front. Moreover, we must ask whether certain Evangelicals are not guilty of confusing the supernatural with the superstitious at this point; for whilst it is true that the classic Evangelical position does indeed involve this commitment to 'supernatural, biblical beliefs', it is also true that the Anglo-Catholic position involves a commitment to superstitious, unbiblical beliefs. Are these Evangelicals happy, we ask, with the 'sacramental system'? Are they happy with the concept of baptismal regeneration and of the Real Presence of Christ? Are they happy with altars, and priests, and ritual? Are they not troubled by the concept of 'God's unwritten word', and the notion of 'catholic consent'? Again, are they happy with the Catholic doctrine of 'Reserve' and the virtual neglect of the preaching of the Word? Are they really happy with the Anglo-Catholic doctrine of justification and with the denial of the principles of *sola scriptura*, *sola gratia* and *sola fide*? And if they are *not* happy in these areas, then are these issues really so minimal and so trivial that they amount to a disagreement of only one-tenth of the whole? There is, without doubt, a strange malaise afloat amongst those Evangelicals whose attitude towards Anglo-Catholicism is one of deference, deep respect, concession, and capitulation. The Grove booklet *Anglo-Catholic Worship* is a prime example of such a malaise. It is essentially an historical survey of various aspects of Anglo-Catholicism, and offers no real critique of a biblical or theological nature. There is an evasion of the real, fundamental doctrinal issues, and the Protestant note which characterized a former generation of Anglican Evangelicals is conspicuously absent. Indeed, it appears to be the case that certain Evangelicals today have lost all capacity for polemical theology with regard to Catholicism; indeed, it appears that the only polemic that has survived in such circles is the polemic against polemics! Let us never forget, then, that the Eternal Son of God did not shrink from polemics when he contended that the Pharisees had made the Word of God of none effect through their traditions. Let us never forget that the great Apostle Paul did not shrink from polemics when he contended that the Galatians had been bewitched by 'another gospel, which is not another'. Let us never forget that the people of God are urged in the Word of God to 'contend earnestly for the faith once delivered unto the saints'.[52]

However, the spirit which is afloat amongst certain Anglican Evangelicals today is one which appears all too often to pay greater deference to the fact of 'Anglican comprehensiveness' and the interests of visible unity than to the truth of the Word of God. Julian Charley, for instance, actually warns in *Rome, Canterbury, and the Future* that 'there is a danger in endeavouring to be a little more precise than the fact of comprehensiveness will allow'. Ecumenical activity, it seems, requires a cult of imprecision, indecisiveness, and vagueness; it requires, apparently, the concept of 'elasticity' and the cult of ambiguity. It requires statements such as that on Eucharistic Doctrine in *The Final Report* to the effect that the members of Christ 'enter into the movement of his self-offering'. Indeed, ecumenical activity in the realm of doctrine requires very often a spirit and an atmosphere which is one of ambiguity, subtlety, confusion, obscurity, contradiction, mystification, and fog! It requires the kind of approach which John Henry Newman described with such brilliant irony in the last century, and which can be charged upon certain Evangelicals today. 'In the present day', wrote Newman,

> mistiness is the mother of wisdom. A man who can set down a half-a-dozen general propositions, which escape from destroying one another only by being diluted into truisms, who can hold the balance between opposites so skilfully as to do without fulcrum or beam, who never enunciates a truth without guarding himself against being supposed to exclude the contradictory,—who holds that Scripture is the only authority, yet that the Church is to be deferred to, that faith only justifies, yet that it does not justify without works, that grace does not depend on the sacraments, yet is not given without them, that bishops are a divine ordinance, yet those who have them not are in the same religious condition as those who have,—this is your safe man and the hope of the Church; this is what the Church is said to want, not party men, but sensible, temperate, sober, well-judging persons, to guide it through the channel of no-meaning, between the Scylla and Charybdis of Aye and No.

John Henry Newman has given us here a perfect description of the tactic of the modern ecumenical mind. It is in evidence in *Growing into Union*; it is in evidence in *The Final Report*— this subtle steering through 'the channel of no-meaning, between the Scylla and Charybdis of Aye and No'. It is a tragic thing when the great truths of the Holy Word of God are handled in this way, and when the Church itself begins to speak with the voice of the oracle of Delphi! [53]

It is evident, then, that the issues of the Oxford Movement of 150 years ago are most relevant today. Leading Evangelicals are pitching their tent toward Oxford—they are pitching their tent toward Rome; and the Tiber is now beginning to flow within Evangelicalism itself. Leading Evangelicals have put themselves into the position of Esau and are bartering and squandering their great heritage for a mere mess of pottage! They are engaged in that 'vanity of vanities'—ecumenical negotiation on God's unchangeable truth. The Protestant note within Evangelicalism has been rapidly ebbing away in recent years, and one of the greatest and most urgent needs within Evangelicalism today is the recovery of that Protestant note. It must not be a cheap Protestantism—it must not be a carnal Protestantism; it must be an intelligent, cogent, spiritual Protestantism—the Protestantism of those great masters of historical theology, Dr William Cunningham and Dr Merle d'Aubigné. It must reassert fearlessly the great principles of the Protestant Reformation—*sola scriptura*, *sola gratia* and *sola fide*. It must protest at the damnable plus of both Anglo-Catholicism and Roman Catholicism. It must never tire of demonstrating that the epistles to the Galatians and to the Hebrews deliver a crushing death-blow to the pallid 'gospel' of Catholicism, exposing that 'gospel' as 'another gospel, which is not another'. It must never cease to warn men of the spiritual bondage into which Catholicism would fain bring them; it must never cease to declare the spiritual liberty which is in Christ Jesus. It must ever proclaim the glorious perfection not only of the Person of Jesus Christ, but also of His Work—that a full and perfect atonement was made once and for all at Calvary—that the Work of Christ is a gloriously finished work—it is a work of pure gold and will not brook the dross of the additions of men. This Evangelical Protestantism must declare from the Scriptures that 'we *have* an altar'—it is the altar of the Cross of Calvary, of 'Jesus

48

Christ, and him crucified'. It must declare that 'we *have* a great high priest, that is passed into the heavens, Jesus the Son of God', and that we are 'complete in him'. What need is there, then, for the sacramental principle or the sacerdotal practice of Catholicism? What need is there for the traditions of men or the weak and beggarly elements of this world? These additions of man are but an insult to the perfect work of Christ and to His perfect written Word, and their effect is to make the Word of God and the work of Christ of none effect. Let those, then, that are Evangelicals ensure that they do not let slip their great Protestant heritage. Let them be strong and of a good courage—let them, like Latimer and Ridley, be strong, and play the man. Let them lift up their voices like trumpets in protest against the 'gospel' of Catholicism which so frustrates the grace of God, and let them declare faithfully and fearlessly the everlasting and unchangeable gospel of Christ who by His 'one sacrifice for sins for ever' is able 'to save them to the uttermost that come unto God by him'.[54]

REFERENCES

1. J. H. Newman, *Apologia pro Vita Sua* (Sheed & Ward, 1982), p.51.
2. O. Chadwick, *The Mind of the Oxford Movement* (A. & C. Black, 1960), p.14; J. Keble, *National Apostasy* (Oxford: J. H. Parker, 1833), p.16; A. R. Vidler, *The Church in an Age of Revolution* (Penguin, 1977), pp.50,49; Keble, *National Apostasy*, p.26.
3. Newman, *Apologia*, p.23; Vidler, *Age of Revolution*, p.50; B. M. G. Reardon, *Religious Thought in the Victorian Age* (Longman, 1980), p.97.
4. Newman, *Apologia*, pp.8, 25-6.
5. Newman, *Apologia*, p.8; Vidler, *Age of Revolution*, p.45.
6. Newman, *Apologia*, p.193; O. Chadwick, *The Secularization of the European Mind in the Nineteenth Century* (CUP, 1977), p.27; Newman, *Apologia,* pp.129,191,20,80.
7. Newman, *Apologia*, pp.129,91.
8. Newman, *Apologia*, p.21; Acts 17:11.
9. Newman, *Apologia*, pp.66,65,66.
10. D. Newsome, *Two Classes of Men* (John Murray, 1974), p.13; Chadwick, *Oxford Movement*, p.55; *The Oxford Book of English Romantic Verse* (OUP, 1958), pp.89-90; Willi Apel, the American musicologist.
11. Newsome, *Two Classes*, pp.33,68.
12. Annotation in the margin of his copy of Wordsworth's *Poems,* vol. 1 (London, 1815), p.viii—see G. Keynes (ed.), *Blake: Complete Writings with Variant Readings* (OUP, 1969), p.782.
13. Newsome, *Two Classes,* pp.22,36; Newman, *Apologia*, p.12; Newsome, *Two Classes*, p.70; Chadwick, *Oxford Movement*, p.18; Newsome, *Two Classes*, p.57.
14. Newman, *Apologia*, p.112; Chadwick, *Oxford Movement*, p.64.
15. Newman, *Apologia*, p.65.
16. Newman, *Apologia*, p.6; W. Cunningham, *Historical Theology*, vol. 1 (Banner of Truth, 1979), p.186; Chadwick, *Oxford Movement*, pp.123,125.
17. J. H. Merle d'Aubigné, *Geneva and Oxford* (London: W. H. Dalton, 1843), p.22; Chadwick, *Oxford Movement*, pp.127,130.
18. Chadwick, *Oxford Movement*, p.127.
19. P. Toon, *Evangelical Theology 1833-1856: A Response to Tractarianism,* (Marshall, Morgan & Scott, 1979), p.126; Newman, *Apologia,* p.76; Toon, *Evangelical Theology*, p.126.
20. J. Pelikan, *The Emergence of the Catholic Tradition* (University of Chicago Press, 1971), pp.336-7; d'Aubigné, *Geneva and Oxford*, p.23.
21. W. G. T. Shedd, *A History of Christian Doctrine*, vol. 2 (Klock & Klock, 1978), pp.440,441-2.
22. Toon, *Evangelical Theology*, p.141; Newman, *Apologia*, pp.3,4,20.

23. C. S. Dessain, *The Rediscovery of Newman: An Oxford Symposium*, (Sheed & Ward/SPCK, 1967), pp.111, 121; Newman, *Apologia*, p.48.
24. J. Buchanan, *The Doctrine of Justification* (Banner of Truth, 1961), p.228; Cunningham, *Historical Theology*, vol. 2, pp.134,123.
25. Galatians 2:16; Buchanan, *Doctrine of Justification*, p.229; O. Chadwick, *Newman* (OUP, 1983), p.12; Newsome, *Two Classes*, pp.72,47,41,42; Galatians 1:6-7; Buchanan, *Doctrine of Justification*, pp.229-30.
26. Newman, *Apologia*, pp.80,33; d'Aubigné, *Geneva and Oxford*, pp.46, 47,49-50; *The Times*, 4 June 1982, p.8.
27. D'Aubigné, *Geneva and Oxford*, p.53; Cunningham, *Historical Theology*, vol. 2, pp.141-2.
28. O. Chadwick, *The Victorian Church*, part 1 (A. & C. Black, 1971), p.175; Reardon, *Religious Thought*, p.95; d'Aubigné, *Geneva and Oxford*, p.13; Newman, *Apologia*, pp.29,35,36; Vidler, *Age of Revolution*, p.45ff.
29. Newman, *Apologia*, pp.46,90,58,148,57,53; Newman, Introduction to Tract 90; Newman, *Apologia*, p.87.
30. Newman, *Apologia*, pp.90,57,53; Newman, Introduction to Tract 90.
31. John 10:35.
32. Newman, *Apologia*, pp.93,109,100,138; Reardon, *Religious Thought*, p.101; Newman, *Apologia*, p.99.
33. Toon, *Evangelical Theology*, p.21; D. Newsome, *The Parting of Friends* (John Murray, 1966), p.14; Chadwick, *Oxford Movement*, p.27.
34. Toon, *Evangelical Theology*, pp.2,44,32-3.
35. D'Aubigné, *Geneva and Oxford,* pp.11,20,56,12,54. Merle d'Aubigné's lecture is now very difficult to obtain, and well deserves to be reprinted.
36. Toon, *Evangelical Theology*, pp.53-4.
37. W. Cunningham, 'Newman on Development', *North British Review*, V (1846), pp.452-3,418. Cunningham's article is excellent and deserves to be reprinted.
38. Newman, *Apologia*, pp.154,155; ibid., Note E, 'The Anglican Church', p.219.
39. Cunningham, 'Newman on Development', p.420.
40. D.Parkes, 'The Beauty of Holiness', in C. Buchanan (ed.), *Anglo-Catholic Worship: An Evangelical Appreciation after 150 years* (Bramcote Notts, 1983), p.36; Chadwick, *The Victorian Church*, part 1, p.213.
41. Chadwick, *Oxford Movement*, pp.27,64; Chadwick, *The Victorian Church,* part 1, p.214; *Oxford Book of English Romantic Verse*, pp.660-2.
42. Toon, *Evangelical Theology*, p.67; d'Aubigné, *Geneva and Oxford*, p.61; J. C. Ryle, *Five English Reformers* (Banner of Truth, 1965), p.36.
43. Buchanan, *Anglo-Catholic Worship*, p.8; *Growing into Union* (SPCK, 1970), p.8.
44. Newman, *The Development of Christian Doctrine* (Sheed & Ward,

1960), pp.54,123; *Growing into Union*, pp.31,32.

45. Newman, *Development*, pp.68-9.

46. Cunningham, 'Newman on Development', p.447.

47. *Growing into Union*, p.55.

48. *The Final Report* (CTS/SPCK, 1982), p.71.

49. *The Final Report*, pp.64,65; J. Charley, *Rome, Canterbury, and the Future* (Bramcote Notts, 1982), p.3.

50. *The Final Report*, p.14; Charley, *Rome, Canterbury, and the Future*, pp.5,7,4,5.

51. J. Stott & T. Dudley-Smith, *Evangelical Anglicans and the ARCIC Final Report: An Assessment and Critique* (Bramcote Notts, 1982), pp.4,2.

52. Buchanan, *Anglo-Catholic Worship*, pp.4,8,3; *Church of England Newspaper*, 15 April 1983, pp.3,1; Galatians 1:6-7; Jude 3.

53. Buchanan, *Anglo-Catholic Worship*, p.8; Charley, *Rome, Canterbury, and the Future*, p.28; *Final Report*, p.14; Newman, *Apologia*, p.69.

54. Galatians 1:6-7; Hebrews 13:10; 1 Corinthians 2:2; Hebrews 4:14; Colossians 2:10; Hebrews 10:12; Hebrews 7:25.